THE

CAT LOVER'S
TREASURY

THE
CAT LOVER'S
TREASURY

Witty and enjoyable writings in praise of cats

Compiled by Charlotte Gerlings

To Mr Ken
– longest whiskers, loudest voice

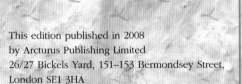

This edition published in 2008
by Arcturus Publishing Limited
26/27 Bickels Yard, 151–153 Bermondsey Street,
London SE1 3HA

In Canada published for Indigo Books
468 King St W,
Suite 500,
Toronto,
Ontario M5V 1L8

Copyright © 2008 Arcturus Publishing Limited

ISBN: 978-1-84193-839-4

Printed in China

Contents

Introduction

A cat purring on our knee as we sit beside the fire; weaving its greeting round our ankles when we come home after work; stretching full length in a patch of sun in the garden; all these scenes will be familiar to that one-fifth of householders in the westernized world who are also cat owners. Yet a pet cat is the nearest thing to a wild animal that we'll ever take into our homes. No sooner has an adorable kitten been placed in our hands than we learn all about its sharp little teeth and claws. Those luminous eyes belong to a born hunter, just as the hectic games of chase and ambush are the sort that any fierce jungle animal would recognize. Millions of us confidently set about taming and training these fascinating animals; we give them names and – more importantly – food; in return they become pleasing companions, and even add a touch of elegance to our lives.

Ailurophilia is the single word that defines the love of cats; it admits people to a unique community whose members share their mutual joys and frustrations. Everything, from furballs and fussy eating to the wonderfully soothing effect of stroking a cat, is understood. This book has been compiled as a tribute to domestic

The cat is the animal to whom the Creator gave the biggest eye, the softest fur, the most supremely delicate nostrils, a mobile ear, an unrivalled paw and a curved claw borrowed from the rose-tree.

SIDONIE-GABRIELLE COLETTE

Best of Friends (1894)
HENRIETTE RONNER-KNIP
(1821–1909)

cats everywhere and as a gift to their devoted owners.

The illustrations have been chosen from many sources, each one a testimony to our long and universal association with cats, which quite possibly began with the Egyptians around 3000BCE. You will find pictures from China, Japan, Russia and India; a Tudor portrait appears alongside 20th-century photo-journalism; Rousseau and Renoir rub shoulders with well-known children's book illustrators and Victorian advertising art.

Numerous writers, artists and musicians have been inspired by cats: T.S. Eliot, Ernest Hemingway, Mark Twain, Colette, Louis Wain, Rossini, Tchaikovsky, Chopin and Ravel, to name just a few.

Each spread of this cat lover's companion includes not only a picture but also something written about cats, ranging from poetry, proverbs and witty quotations to feline adventure tales; thus completing the tribute to these beautiful, affectionate and enigmatic creatures.

The smallest feline is a masterpiece.

LEONARDO DA VINCI

Cats and Children

The pussy cat makes frequent appearances in children's stories and rhymes, and not always in a heroic or flattering role, yet this prevalence shows what a firm niche the cat has occupied in the domestic scene for centuries.

Pictures of children and cats together generally make a charming combination, although cats were sometimes included in portraits as a hint of the wildness of nature sitting alongside the innocence of childhood. Parents – and the cats themselves – might well think otherwise.

The Senses: Touch (1907)
JESSIE WILLCOX SMITH
(1863–1935)

St Jerome's Cat

ANONYMOUS

St Jerome in his study kept a great big cat,

it's always in his pictures, with its feet upon the mat.

Did he give it milk to drink, in a little dish?

When it came to Fridays, did he give it fish?

If I lost my little cat, I'd be sad without it;

I should ask St Jerome what to do about it.

I should ask St Jerome, just because of that,

for he's the only saint I know who kept a kitty cat.

Pussy's Picture (1887)
HARRIETT M. BENNETT
(born *c*.1850)

Puss in Boots

Adapted from the tale by CHARLES PERRAULT (1628–1703)

A POOR MILLER died, leaving everything to his three sons. The oldest inherited the mill, the second his father's donkey, but the youngest boy got only the cat. At first, he feared both he and Puss would starve. *The cat, however, asked for a bag and a pair of boots and set off, vowing that all would be well.*

Puss soon caught a plump rabbit but instead of returning to the boy, he took it to the king, saying that it was a present from his master, the Marquis of Carabas – a name he made up on the spot. After that, CLEVER PUSS caught more and more game for the king, each time offering it with the same message.

One day, the king went riding in his coach with his daughter down beside the river, where Puss had told the boy to go for a swim. While he was in the water, Puss hid his ragged shirt and trousers, and then called out to the king as he passed that thieves had made off with his master's clothes.

'*Puss hid his ragged shirt and trousers, and
then called out to the king*'

Help! (1867)
GUSTAVE DORÉ
(1832–83)

Illustration from *The Terrible
Raminagrobis and the Mice (19th century)*

The KING quickly sent a servant to fetch some new clothes fit for a marquis. *Dressed like a lord*, the boy joined the king and the princess in their coach. Puss ran ahead and ordered everyone to say that the land they were working on belonged to the Marquis of Carabas. And so the king thought that the boy must be very rich indeed. Away in the distance, beyond the fields, stood a castle owned by a wealthy OGRE. Puss bravely marched up and knocked on the castle door. There he asked the ogre if it was true that he could turn himself into any sort of animal in the world. The ogre said '*Yes*' and, to prove it, he changed first into a lion and then an elephant. Puss then challenged the ogre to turn himself into something tiny, like a MOUSE. The foolish ogre did so – whereupon the cat promptly ate him up.

When the coach bearing the king, the princess and the boy arrived at the castle, Puss announced that it belonged to the Marquis of Carabas. The king was so impressed that he agreed happily to the marriage of the boy and the princess, who had fallen in love with each other at first sight.

Hey diddle diddle,
The cat and the fiddle,
The cow jumped over
    the moon;
The little dog laughed,
    To see such craft
And the dish ran away
    with the spoon.

Pussy Cat, Pussy Cat

Pussy Cat, Pussy Cat, where have you been?

I've been to London to look at the Queen.

Pussy Cat, Pussy Cat, what did you there?

I frighten'd a little mouse under the chair.

Three Little Kittens

This nursery rhyme first appeared in
The Only True Mother Goose Melodies (1843)

Three little kittens they lost their mittens, and
they began to cry,
'Oh mother dear, we sadly fear our mittens we
have lost.'
'What! Lost your mittens, you naughty kittens!
Then you shall have no pie.'
'Meeow, meeow, now we shall have no pie.'

Three little kittens they found their mittens, and they
began to cry,
'Oh mother dear, see here, see here, our mittens we
have found.'
'What! Found your mittens, you clever kittens
Now you shall have some pie'
'Meeow, meeow, now let us have some pie.'

Three Little Kittens (1930)
CLARA M. BURD
(1873–1933)

'Oh mother dear, we sadly fear

our mittens we have lost'

I Love Little Pussy (c.1830)

I love little Pussy,

    her coat is so warm,

And if I don't hurt her,

    she'll do me no harm.

So I'll not pull her tail,

    nor drive her away,

But Pussy and I

    together will stay.

She'll sit by my side

    and I'll give her some food,

And Pussy will love me

    because I am good.

I Love Little Pussy postcard (c.1920)

I Have a Cat

A playschool rhyme with actions: chant each line slowly (and the children echo)

I have a cat (I have a cat)
  (Cross arms in front and wiggle fingers like whiskers)

My cat is fat (My cat is fat)
  (Hold arms out in a circle at stomach level)

I have a cat (I have a cat)
  (Cross arms in front and wiggle fingers like whiskers)

My cat wears a hat (My cat wears a hat)
  (Raise arms and touch fingertips over head)

I have a cat (I have a cat)
  (Cross arms in front and wiggle fingers like whiskers)

My cat caught a bat (My cat caught a bat)
  (Hands in front, one on top of the other, fluttering fingers)

I have a cat (I have a cat)
  (Cross arms in front and wiggle fingers like whiskers)

MEOW!

Whisky in the dolls' pram, 1954
PRIVATE COLLECTION

The House that Jack Built

Nursery rhyme first popularized by RANDOLPH CALDECOTT (1846–86)

This is the house that Jack built.

This is the malt

That lay in the house that Jack built.

This is the rat,

That ate the malt

That lay in the house that Jack built.

This is the cat,

That killed the rat,

That ate the malt

That lay in the house that Jack built.

The English artist, Randolph Caldecott (1846–86), illustrated a whole series of children's books, including this picture for The House that Jack Built *(1878). The Ralph Caldecott Medal is awarded annually by the Children's Division of the American Library Association, 'to the artist of the most distinguished American picture book for children' produced in that year.*

Poems in Praise of Cats

The oldest poem in this selection dates from the 9th century and we can guess that, quite apart from its accepted function in vermin control, the domestic cat very soon managed to work its way deep into the affections of our early ancestors.

Poetry, like music, has the power to represent our emotions, so these poems are as much about ourselves – our passions, fears and desires – as the many and various cats who appear in their verses.

Girl with Kitten (1745)
JEAN-BAPTISTE PERRONNEAU
(*c*.1745–83)

The Kitten and
the Falling Leaves (1807)

An extract from a poem by WILLIAM WORDSWORTH (1770–1850)

See the kitten on the wall,

sporting with the leaves that fall.

Withered leaves – one – two – and three

from the lofty elder tree! ...

Each invisible and mute,

In his wavering parachute.

– But the Kitten, how she starts,

crouches, stretches, paws, and darts!

First at one, and then its fellow

just as light and just as yellow;

There are many now – now one –

Now they stop and there are none. ...

Were her antics played in the eye

of a thousand standers-by,

clapping hands with shout and stare,

what would little Tabby care

For the plaudits of the crowd?

Over happy to be proud,

Over wealthy in the treasure

Of her own exceeding pleasure!

Cat on a Wall (1914)
CECIL ALDIN
(1870–1935)

The Retired Cat (1791)

An extract from a poem by WILLIAM COWPER *(1731–1800)*

A poet's cat, sedate and grave,
As poet well could wish to have,
Was much addicted to inquire,
For nooks to which she might retire,
And where, secure as mouse in chink,
She might repose, or sit and think.
I know not where she caught her trick —
Nature perhaps herself had cast her,
In such a mould *philosophique*,
Or else she learn'd it of her master.
Sometimes ascending, debonair,
An apple tree or lofty pear,
Lodg'd with convenience in the fork,
She watched the gard'ner at his work;
Sometimes her ease and solace sought,
In an old empty wat'ring-pot,
There, wanting nothing save a fan,
To seem some nymph in her sedan,
Apparell'd in exactest sort,
And ready to be borne to court.

Cat (1747)
SHEN QUAN
(1682–1762)

To Mrs Reynolds's Cat (1818)

by JOHN KEATS (1795–1821)

Cat! who hast pass'd thy grand climacteric,
How many mice and rats hast in thy days

Destroy'd? – How many tidbits stolen? Gaze

With those bright languid segments green, and prick

Those velvet ears – but pr'ythee do not stick

Thy latent talons in me – and upraise

Thy gentle mew – and tell me all thy frays

Of fish and mice, and rats and tender chick.

Nay, look not down, nor lick thy dainty wrists –

For all the wheezy asthma – and for all

Thy tail's tip is nick'd off – and though the fists

Of many a maid have given thee many a maul,

Still is that fur as soft as when the lists

In youth thou enter'dst on glass-bottled wall.

'How many mice and rats hast in thy days destroy'd?'

Tabby Cat (1874)
WILLIAM HUGGINS
(1820–84)

Milk for the Cat

An extract from the poem by HAROLD MUNRO (1879–1932)

The white saucer like some full moon descends
at last from the cloud of the table above;
she sighs and dreams and thrills and glows,
transfigured with love.

She nestles over the shining rim,
buries her chin in the creamy sea;
her tail hangs loose; each drowsy paw
is doubled under each bending knee.

A long dim ecstasy holds her life;
her world is an infinite shapeless white,
till her tongue has curled the last holy drop;
then she sinks back into the night.

Draws and dips her body to heap
her sleepy nerves in the great arm-chair,
lies defeated and buried deep
three or four hours unconscious there.

*Kitty's Breakfast
(1883)*
EMILY FARMER
(1828–1905)

A Cat

by EDWARD THOMAS (1878–1917)

She had a name among the children;
But no one loved though someone owned
Her, locked her out of doors at bedtime
And had her kittens duly drowned.

In Spring, nevertheless, this cat
Ate blackbirds, thrushes, nightingales,
And birds of bright voice and plume and flight,
As well as scraps from neighbours' pails.

I loathed and hated her for this;
One speckle on a thrush's breast
Was worth a million such; and yet
She lived long, till God gave her rest.

The Afternoon Nap
Jules Gasson
(1853–1924)

'This cat ate blackbirds, thrushes, nightingales,
And birds of bright voice and plume and flight'

She Sights a Bird – She Chuckles (1862)

by EMILY DICKINSON (1830–86)

She sights a Bird – she chuckles –
She flattens – then she crawls –
She runs without the look of feet –
Her eyes increase to Balls –
Her Jaws stir – twitching – hungry –
Her Teeth can hardly stand –
She leaps, but Robin leaped the first –
Ah, Pussy, of the Sand,
The Hopes so juicy ripening –
You almost bathed your Tongue –
When Bliss disclosed a hundred Toes –
And fled with every one.

Grey Cat Ready To Pounce (1900)
MURIEL I. HUNT
(1883–1973)

Familiarity Dangerous

translated by WILLIAM COWPER (1731–1800)

from a Latin poem by VINCENT BOURNE (1695–1747)

As in her ancient mistress' lap
The youthful tabby lay,
They gave each other many a tap,
Alike disposed to play.

But strife ensues. Puss waxes warm,
And with protruded claws
Ploughs all the length of Lydia's arm,
Mere wantonness the cause.

At once, resentful of the deed,
She shakes her to the ground
With many a threat that she shall bleed
With still a deeper wound.

But, Lydia, bid thy fury rest:
It was a venial stroke:
For she that will with kittens jest
Should bear a kitten's joke.

'She that will with kittens jest should bear a kitten's joke'

Tabby Cat (early 18th century)
PRIVATE COLLECTION

Pangur Ban

In the 9th century, an Irish monk revealed his love for his little white cat in a poem he wrote in the margins of a manuscript.

I and Pangur Ban, my cat,
'Tis a like task we are at;
Hunting mice is his delight,
Hunting words I sit all night.

'Tis a merry thing to see
At our task how glad are we,
When at home we sit and find
Entertainment to our mind.

Oftentimes a mouse will stray
In the hero Pangur's way;
Oftentimes my keen thought set
Takes a meaning in its net.

The Cat
HENRI GAUDIER-BRZESKA
(1891–1915)

'Gainst the wall he sets his eye
Full and fierce and sharp and sly;
'Gainst the wall of knowledge I
All my little wisdom try.

When a mouse darts from its den.
O how glad is Pangur then!
O what gladness do I prove
When I solve the doubts I love!

Practice every day has made
Pangur perfect in his trade;
I get wisdom day and night,
Turning darkness into light.

To a Cat (1893)

An extract from a poem by ALGERNON CHARLES SWINBURNE
(1837–1909)

Stately, kindly, lordly friend,
Condescend

Here to sit by me, and turn

Glorious eyes that smile and burn,

Golden eyes, love's lustrous meed,

On the golden page I read.

All your wondrous wealth of hair,

Dark and fair,

Silken-shaggy, soft and bright

As the clouds and beams of night,

Pays my reverent hand's caress

Back with friendlier gentleness.

Dogs may fawn on all and some

As they come;

You, a friend of loftier mind,

Answer friends alone in kind.

Just your foot upon my hand

Softly bids it understand.

Tortoiseshell Cat (1866)
WILLIAM HUGGINS
(1820–84)

On a Favourite Cat Drowned in a Tub of Goldfishes (1748)

by THOMAS GRAY (1716–71)

This poem, on the death of his cat, was greatly prized by Horace Walpole. After the poet's death, the bowl was placed on a pedestal at Walpole's house in Strawberry Hill, Twickenham, with a few lines from the poem as an inscription.

Kittens and Goldfish Bowl
POSTCARD (1910)

Twas on a lofty vase's side,
Where China's gayest art had dyed
The azure flowers that blow;
Demurest of the tabby kind,
The pensive Selima reclined,
Gazed on the lake below.

Her conscious tail her joy declared;
The fair round face, the snowy beard,
The velvet of her paws,
Her coat that with the tortoise vies,
Her ears of jet, and emerald eyes,
She saw; and purred applause.

Still had she gazed; but 'midst the tide
Two angel forms were seen to glide,
The Genii of the stream;
Their scaly armour's Tyrian hue
Thro' richest purple to the view
Betrayed a golden gleam.

The hapless Nymph with wonder saw:
A whisker first and then a claw,
  With many an ardent wish,
She stretched in vain to reach the prize.
What female heart can gold despise?
  What Cat's averse to fish?

Presumptuous Maid! with looks intent
Again she stretched, again she bent,
  Nor knew the gulf between.
(Malignant Fate sat by, and smiled.)
The slippery verge her feet beguiled,
  She tumbled headlong in.

Eight times emerging from the flood
She mewed to every watery god,
  Some speedy aid to send.
No Dolphin came, no Nereid stirred:
Nor cruel Tom, nor Susan heard.
  A Favourite has no friend!

Comic Sketches (1834)
ROBERT SEYMOUR
(1800–36)

From hence, ye Beauties, undeceived,

Know, one false step is ne'er retrieved,

And be with caution bold.

Not all that tempts your wandering eyes

And heedless hearts, is lawful prize;

Nor all that glisters, gold.

To My Cat (1895)

by ROSAMUND MARRIOTT WATSON (1860–1911)

Half loving-kindliness, and half disdain,
Thou comest to my call serenely suave

With humming speech and gracious gestures grave

In salutation courtly and urbane;

Yet must I humble me thy grace to gain,

For wiles may win thee though no arts enslave,

And nowhere gladly thou abidest save

Where nought disturbs the concord of thy reign.

Sphinx of my quiet hearth! who deign'st to dwell

Friend of my toil, companion of mine ease,

Thine is the lore of Ra and Rameses;

That men forget dost thou remember well,

Beholden still in blinking reveries

With sombre, sea-green gaze inscrutable.

Tabby Cat (2006)
PRIVATE COLLECTION

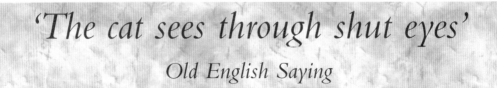

'The cat sees through shut eyes'

Old English Saying

Sayings and Proverbs

The air of mystery that cats have managed to create around themselves has made them prime objects of superstition down the ages. Their shrewd gaze can penetrate anything, it seems; and their elusiveness is legendary.

They are, of course, nocturnal hunters and lovers, as well as our cuddlesome daytime companions. What other domestic creature offers us so much fascination and puzzlement?

Puss Napping (1856)
George Baxter
(1804–67)

Belling the Cat

From the fable by AESOP

A group of mice once held a council to discuss what was to be done about their great enemy, THE CAT. One by one they were being caught and killed, so it was clear that they urgently needed some kind of warning of the cat's approach. One young mouse proposed that they should tie a bell around the creature's neck; then, when they heard the tinkling sound, they could all run away and hide. This idea was greeted with immense enthusiasm; one member of the council knew the whereabouts of a bell and two others offered to gnaw a length of ribbon from the housekeeper's hat. However, when the oldest mouse stood up and asked who would actually tie the bell onto the cat, strangely enough, there was not one among them willing to risk it.

'Just as I thought,' said the old mouse, 'certain things are easier said than done.'

'Just as I thought,' said the old mouse, 'certain things are easier said than done.'

Kitten and Ball of Wool
(1866)
MURATA KOKODA
(1840–98)

Proverbs

❋ A cat has nine lives. For three he plays, for three he strays, and for he last three he stays.
English

❋ A cat may look at a king.
English

❋ A house without either a cat or a dog is the house of a scoundrel.
Portuguese

❋ After dark, all cats are leopards.
Native American

❋ Cats don't catch mice to please God.
Afghan

❋ I gave an order to a cat and the cat gave it to its tail.
Chinese

❋ If stretching were wealth then the cat would be rich.
African

❋ One should not send a cat to deliver cream.
Yiddish

❋ The cat's a saint when there are no mice about.
Japanese

❋ The cat who frightens the mice away is as good as the cat who eats them.
German

❋ Those who dislike cats will be carried to the cemetery in the rain.
Dutch

❋ When the cat's away, the mice will play.
English

❋ When the mouse laughs at the cat, it means there's a hole nearby.
Nigerian

❋ When rats infest the Palace, a lame cat is better than the swiftest horse.
Chinese

The Favourite
WILHELM SCHUTZE
(1840–98)

Dreaming about Cats

✣ Dreaming of a white cat means that you are in love.

✣ Dreaming of a black cat warns of some misfortune about to happen.

✣ To dream of a grey cat means you should follow your ambitions.

✣ To dream of a ginger cat predicts success in business.

✣ To dream of a black and white cat means either that children will bring you luck or that there will be a birth in the family.

✣ If you dream of a tabby cat, you will have a happy home and fortune will smile on all who live there.

✣ Dreaming of more than one cat means that your partner is unfaithful.

✣ To dream of a cat meowing warns against rumours and false friends.

✣ Dreaming of a cat fight signifies a quarrel.

✣ To dream of being scratched by a cat warns against sickness and trouble.

'To dream of a tortoiseshell cat means that you will be lucky in love'

Kittens
GEORGE SHERIDAN KNOWLES
(1863–1931)

About Black Cats

* The Scots believe that a strange black cat on your porch brings prosperity.
* It's very lucky for a black cat to come into a house or aboard ship, and the cat should never be chased away, in case it takes the luck with it.
* In Britain and parts of Europe, it's good luck for a black cat to cross your path.
* There is a popular saying that 'Whenever the cat of the house is black, the lasses of lovers shall have no lack'.

* In England, a black cat crossing the path of the bride as she leaves the church is said to grant a happy marriage.
* Stroking the tail of a black cat will cure a stye in the eye.
* The Irish say that a black cat crossing one's path by moonlight means death in an epidemic.
* A black cat in the audience on the opening night portends a successful play.
* A black cat walking towards you brings good fortune but if it walks away, the luck is removed.

On every black cat there is a single white hair. If you can remove it without the cat scratching you, this white hair will bring you either wealth or luck in love.

Black Cat on Window Sill (1999)
PRIVATE COLLECTION

Cats are...

Cats are ... well, so many things, it is no wonder mere humans are completely captivated by them. The following quotations amount to an anthology of wit and wisdom specially designed for cat lovers, who − it is hoped − will nod, smile and roll their eyes in recognition of their own furry housemates, with every turn of the page.

Playing With a Cat (1897)
Toyohara Chikanobu
(1838–1912)

Comic

There is no more intrepid explorer than a kitten.
He gets himself into every kind of trouble.

JULES CHAMPFLEURY

Kittens believe that all nature is occupied
with their diversion.

F. A. PARADIS DE MONCRIF

If he is comic, it is only because of the incongruity
of so demure a look and so wild a heart.

ALAN DEVOE

A Curious Kitten (1881)
FRANK PATON
(1856–1909)

Endearing

A kitten is in the animal world what a rosebud
is in the garden.
ROBERT SOUTHEY

It is impossible to keep a straight face in the presence of one or more kittens.

CYNTHIA E. VARNADO

The trouble with a kitten is that
Eventually it becomes a cat.
OGDEN NASH

I named my kitten Rose – fur soft as a petal, claws
sharper than thorns.
ASTRID ALAUDA

Kittens Up To Mischief (c.1870)
Horatio Henry Couldery
(1832–c.1893)

Temperamental

One must love a cat on its own terms.

PAUL GRAY

*The man who carries a cat by the tail learns
something that can be learned in no other way.*

MARK TWAIN

*Some people say man is the most dangerous animal on the planet.
Obviously those people have never met an angry cat.*

LILLIAN JOHNSON

*Those who play with cats must
expect to be scratched.*

MIGUEL DE CERVANTES

*Naughty Puss
(late 19th century)*
ADVERTISING IMAGE FOR
JAYNE'S TONIC VERMIFUGE

Aloof

After scolding one's cat, one looks into its face and is seized by the ugly suspicion that it understood every word. And has filed it for reference.

CHARLOTTE GRAY

A cat's got her own opinion of human beings. She don't say much, but you can tell enough to make you anxious not to hear the whole of it.

JEROME K. JEROME

The problem with cats is that they get the exact same look on their face whether they see a moth or an axe-murderer.

PAULA POUNDSTONE

Nobody can give a withering stare quite as crushing as a disdainful cat.

ANONYMOUS

A Domestic Cat (1790)
THOMAS BEWICK
(1753–1828)

Restful

A cat pours his body on the floor like water. It is restful just to see him.

WILLIAM LYON PHELPS

A drowsy winter evening is never quite drowsy enough without a sleeping cat.

ANONYMOUS

Sometimes he curls up on my pillow during the night and I don't know he's there until I yawn and my mouth closes on a whisker.

ASTRID ALAUDA

You cannot look at a sleeping cat and feel tense.

JANE PAULEY

Sleeping Cat (c. 1850)
PRIVATE COLLECTION

Wily

*Some circumstantial evidence is very strong, as when
you find a trout in the milk.*

HENRY DAVID THOREAU

Keep an eye on the cat and another on the frying pan.

PROVERB

*Most of us rather like our cats to have a streak of
wickedness. I should not feel quite easy in the company
of any cat that walked about the house with a
saintly expression.*

BEVERLEY NICHOLS

If cats could talk, they wouldn't.

NAN PORTER

Cat with Fish
KALIGHAT
SCHOOL, INDIA

Curious

Even if you have just destroyed a

Ming vase, purr. Usually all

will be forgiven.

LENNY RUBENSTEIN

It is impossible for a lover of cats to banish
these alert, gentle, and discriminating little
friends, who give us just enough of their
regard and complaisance to make us
hunger for more.

AGNES REPPLIER

Curiosity killed the cat,

Satisfaction brought it back!

ENGLISH PROVERB

Girl with a Cat (1882)
PIERRE AUGUSTE RENOIR
(1841–1919)

Playful

Playing with the Kitten (1876)
Joseph Clark
(1834–1926)

I have noticed that what cats most appreciate in a human being is not the ability to produce food, which they take for granted, but his or her entertainment value.

Anonymous

Of all the toys available, none is better designed than the owner himself. A large multipurpose plaything, its parts can be made to move in almost any direction.

Stephen Baker

Time spent with cats is never wasted.

Sidonie-Gabrielle Colette

When I play with my cat, who knows if I am not a pastime to her more than she is to me?

Michel de Montaigne

Self-assured

*The domestic cat seems to have greater confidence in itself
than in anyone else.*
LAWRENCE N. JOHNSON

*Cats were put into the world
to disprove the dogma that
all things were created to
serve man.*
PAUL GRAY

You own a dog but you feed a cat.
JENNY DE VRIES

*Cats seem to go on the principle that it never does any harm
to ask for what you want.*
JOSEPH WOOD KRUTCH

Don't Forget Us (19th century)
ILLUSTRATION FROM VICTORIAN
CHILDREN'S BOOK

Companionable

Authors like cats because they are such quiet, lovable, wise creatures, and cats like authors for the same reasons.

ROBERTSON DAVIES

If by chance I seated myself to write, she very slyly, very tenderly, seeking protection and caresses, would softly take her place on my knee and follow the comings and goings of my pen – sometimes effacing, with an unintentional stroke of her paw, lines of whose tenor she disapproved.

PIERRE LOTI

Cats are dangerous companions for writers because cat watching is a near-perfect method of writing avoidance.

DAN GREENBURG

Pierre Loti (1891)
HENRI ROUSSEAU
(1844–1910)

Affectionate

Purring would seem to be, in her case, an automatic safety valve device for dealing with happiness overflow.

MONICA EDWARDS

If there were to be a universal sound depicting peace, I would surely vote for the purr.

BARBARA L. DIAMOND

If we treated everyone we meet with the same affection we bestow upon our favourite cat, they, too, would purr.

MARTIN BUXBAUM

A cat will lie the whole evening on your knee, purring and happy in your society.

THEOPHILE GAUTIER

Mademoiselle Julie Manet with Cat (1887)
PIERRE AUGUSTE RENOIR
(1841–1919)

Prolific

One cat just leads to another.
ERNEST HEMINGWAY

Kittens can happen to anyone.
PAUL GALLICO

It's really the cat's house – we
just pay the mortgage.
ANONYMOUS

Most beds sleep up to six cats.
Ten cats without the owner.
STEPHEN BAKER

Mothercare (1898)
HENRIETTE RONNER-KNIP
(1821–1909)

Elegant

*Like a graceful vase, a cat, even when motionless,
seems to flow.*

GEORGE F. WILL

The ideal of calm exists

in a sitting cat.

JULES REYNARD

*Cats can work out mathematically the exact place to sit that will
cause the most inconvenience.*

PAM BROWN

*There's no need for a piece
of sculpture in a home that has a cat.*

WESLEY BATES

Two Decorative Cats (1904)
LUDWIG HOHLWEIN
(1874–1949)

Clever

Although all cat games have their rules and rituals, these vary with the individual player. The cat, of course, never breaks a rule. If it does not follow precedent, that simply means it has created a new rule and it is up to you to learn it quickly if you want the game to continue.

SIDNEY DENHAM

Cats are notoriously sore losers. Coming in second best, especially to someone as poorly coordinated as a human being, grates their sensibility.

STEPHEN BAKER

It's very hard to be polite if you're a cat.

ANONYMOUS

Cats have an infallible understanding of total concentration — and get between you and it.

ARTHUR BRIDGES

The Game of Chess (19th century)
PRIVATE COLLECTION

Serene

There has never been a cat

Who couldn't calm me down

By walking slowly

Past my chair.

Rod McKuen

I love cats because I love my home and after a while they become its visible soul.

Jean Cocteau

I believe cats to be spirits come to earth. A cat, I am sure, could walk on a cloud without coming through.

Jules Verne

There is something about the presence of a cat ... that seems to take the bite out of being alone.

Louis J. Camuti

Henriette Ronner.

Studies of Cats (1895)
HENRIETTE RONNER-KNIP
(1821–1909)

Two White Persian Cats With a Ladybird (1900)
ARTHUR HEYER
(1872–1931)

Cats from Literature and Letters

This part of the book offers only a glimpse of the range of writing about cats; and so many writers turn out to be cat owners that it is not possible to mention them all. One clue to their compatibility is that the feline attributes of unhurried contemplation and the ability to stay focused will benefit the writer too.

In addition, writing is a solitary job, and the blank sheet of paper is not nearly so daunting if one's own Hodge or Foss is already curled up on it.

Take a Cat

from **The Manciple's Tale**
by GEOFFREY CHAUCER (1386–1400)

Take a cat, and nourish him well with milk

And tender meat, make him a couch of silk,

But let him see a mouse creep out the wall,

And he'll abandon milk and meat and all,

And every dainty morsel in the house,

Such appetite has he to eat a mouse.

Cat and Mouse (1996)
FRANCES MIDDENDORF

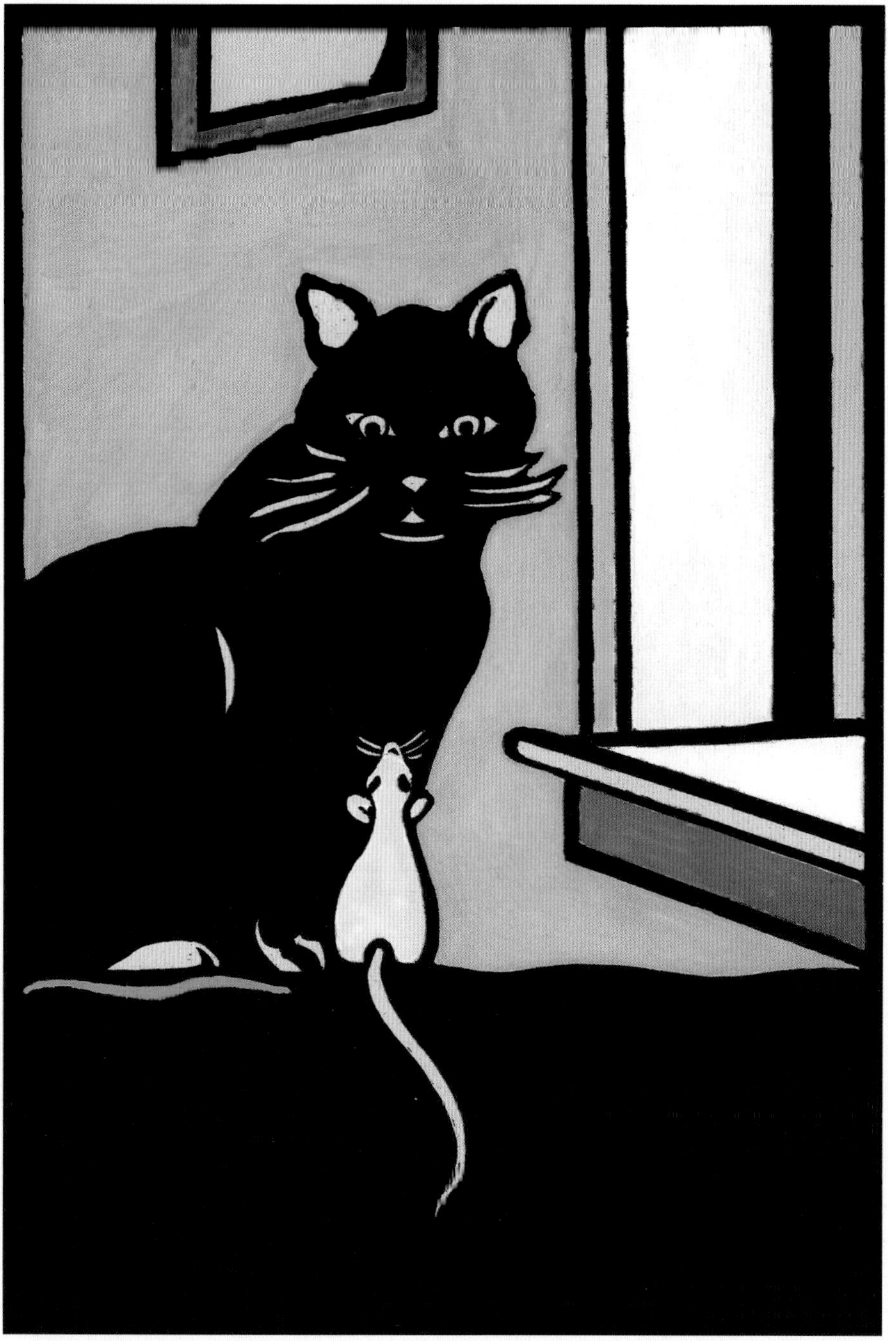

A Very Fine Cat Indeed

from *The Life of Samuel Johnson* *(1791)*

by JAMES BOSWELL (1740–95)

I never shall forget the INDULGENCE with which he treated HODGE, his cat: for whom he himself used to go out and buy OYSTERS, lest the servants having that trouble should take a dislike to the poor creature.

I recollect him one day scrambling up Dr Johnson's breast, apparently with much satisfaction, while my friend smiling and half-whistling, rubbed down his back, and pulled him by the tail; and when I observed he was a fine cat, saying, '*Why yes, Sir, but I have had cats whom I liked better than this*'; and then as if perceiving Hodge to be out of countenance, adding, '*but he is a very fine cat, a very fine cat indeed*'.

Minnie (1876)
R.P. Thrall

Florence Nightingale and Her Cats

Florence Nightingale (1820–1910) owned sixty cats during her lifetime. They were all Persians and she often named them after famous men of the day, such as Disraeli, Gladstone and Bismarck. Cats figure large in Nightingale's correspondence and inky paw marks sometimes track across her notepaper.

White Persian Cat (1877)
HARRISON WILLIAM WEIR
(1824–1906)

Dearest Madame Mohl

Could you recommend me a home for Mr Muff at once? He is quite too troublesome to keep. And he is very unhappy, poor fellow (And I have had quite too much of policemen, and printing Hand Bills, & offering rewards, & paying them, for lost or stolen Tom Cats in London).

He is very handsome – thoro'bred, very good natured, about 9 or 10 months old – I am very sorry to part with him.

(16 JULY 1870)

Dearest Madame Mohl

The Tom Kitten with a 'pretty face', which you said you would like when you were here has been scrupulously set apart for you.

He has now, I think, the longest hair I ever saw: is most affectionate & very clean … his name is Biz … I should think he would be greatly admired even in Paris: If he stops here he will be stolen or lost …

(20 JANUARY 1877)

Foss

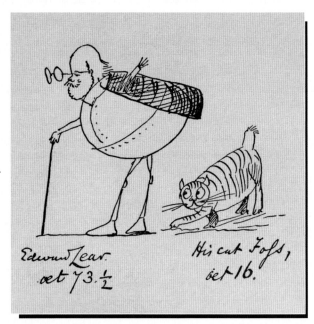

This drawing, *Edward Lear Aged 73-and-a-half and His Cat Foss Aged 16*, was produced by Lear in 1885. It shows his celebrated pet cat,

who joined the household in 1872. FOSS WAS A LARGE, ROUND TABBY with a shortened tail, cut down to a stump by an ignorant servant to prevent the animal from straying.

Foss was definitely no beauty, but he became well-known through numerous CARTOONS drawn by his master. The only attempt to photograph him ended in failure when he sprang from Lear's arms as the camera shutter came down.

*Edward Lear Aged 73-and-a-half
and his Cat Foss Aged 16 (1885)*
EDWARD LEAR (1812–88)

Consequently, 'the Foss we know belongs more to the world of nonsense stories and songs than he does to the real world.'

Lear was a gifted bird, animal and landscape artist who led a nomadic existence, always in search of new and exotic material for his work. He travelled – among other places – to Sicily, Egypt, Malta and Corfu, and finally settled with Foss at San Remo, Italy. Because he loved the cat so much, he instructed the architects of his new house in San Remo to design it as an exact replica of his previous one, to make the move to the new place as easy as possible for Foss.

FOSS DIED IN NOVEMBER OF 1887, and was laid to rest under a large stone in Lear's Italian garden. *Lear himself died only two months later, in January 1888.*

In the Duchess's Kitchen

from *Alice's Adventures in Wonderland* *(1865)*

by LEWIS CARROLL (1832–98)

The only things in the kitchen that did not sneeze, were the COOK, and a LARGE CAT which was sitting on the hearth and grinning from ear to ear.

'*Please would you tell me,*' said Alice, a little timidly, for she was not quite sure whether it was good manners for her to speak first, '*why your cat grins like that?*'

'*It's a Cheshire cat,*' said the Duchess, '*and that's why. Pig!*'

She said the last word with such sudden violence that Alice quite jumped; but she saw in another moment that it was addressed to the baby, and not to her, so she took courage, and went on again:

'*I didn't know that Cheshire cats always grinned; in fact, I didn't know that cats could grin.*'

'*They all can,*' said the Duchess; '*and most of 'em do.*'

'*I don't know of any that do,*' Alice said very politely, feeling quite pleased to have got into a conversation.

'*You don't know much,*' said the Duchess; '*and that's a fact.*'

An Excited Cat (1916)
LOUIS WAIN
(1860–1939)

Dinah and Her Children

from ***Through the Looking-glass*** *(1871)*

by LEWIS CARROLL *(1832–98)*

One thing was certain, that the WHITE KITTEN had nothing to do with it: – it was the black kitten's fault entirely. For the white kitten had been having its face washed by the old cat for the last quarter of an hour (and bearing it pretty well, considering); so you see that it couldn't have had any hand in the mischief.

The way Dinah washed her children's faces was this: *first she held the poor thing down by its ear with one paw, and then with the other paw she rubbed its face all over*, the wrong way, beginning at the nose: and just now, she was hard at work on the white kitten, which was lying quite still and trying to purr – no doubt feeling that it was all meant for its good.

But the BLACK KITTEN had been finished with earlier in the afternoon, and so… had been having a grand game of romps with the ball of worsted Alice had been trying to wind up… and there it was, spread over the hearth-rug, all knots and tangles, with the kitten running after its own tail in the middle.

The Proud Mother
CHARLES VAN DEN EYCKEN
(1859–1923)

When Montmorency Meets a Cat

from *Three Men in a Boat* (1889)
by JEROME K. JEROME (1859–1927)

The only subject on which Montmorency and I have any serious difference of opinion is cats. I LIKE CATS; MONTMORENCY DOES NOT.

When I meet a cat, I say, '*Poor Pussy!*' and stoop down and tickle the side of its head; and the cat sticks up its tail in a rigid, cast-iron manner, arches its back, and wipes its nose up against my trousers; and all is gentleness and peace. *When Montmorency meets a cat, the whole street knows about it*; and there is enough bad language wasted in ten seconds to last an ordinarily respectable man all his life, with care.

Dog Scaring Cat (1870)
UNNAMED ARTIST IN AUNT
LOUISA'S BIRTHDAY GIFT

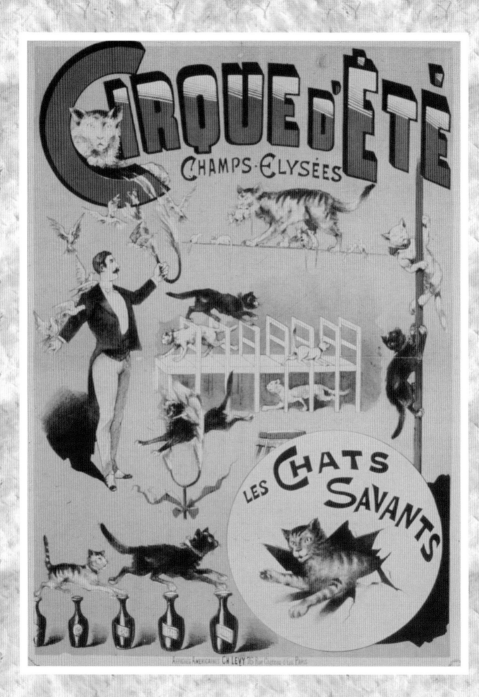

Legends

A miscellany of customs, legends and true-life tales that celebrate the cat as hero, icon and possessor of marvellous powers. Cat-ownership is generally a private affair but, now and again, one particular cat strides into the spotlight and attracts the attention of a wider public. And so fresh legends are made and our admiration continues.

With their qualities of cleanliness, discretion, affection, patience, dignity, and courage, how many of us, I ask you, would be capable of being cats?

FERNAND MERY

Late 19th-century poster for the
Cirque d'Été in Paris

The Japanese Bobtail

'Cat in Window Looking Out at Rice Fields near Asakusa'
from *One Hundred Famous Views of Edo (1857)*
ANDO HIROSHIGE (1797–1858)

HIROSHIGE'S woodcut features one of the distinctive bobtail cats of Japan. The curves or kinks in the tail, responsible for the pompom effect, are unique to each individual cat; just like human finger prints, no two tails are ever alike.

There is a Japanese legend that describes the origins of the bobtail (in reality, the breed has been found in many regions of the Far East). One night, the tail of a sleeping cat was set alight by a spark from a nearby hearth. The terrified cat tore through the streets of the Imperial City, setting every house on fire with its blazing tail. When he surveyed the charred ruins of his city next morning, the Emperor decreed that cats should have their tails trimmed short to prevent a similar disaster. And that is how the first BOBTAILS came about.

For many years in Japan, only the nobility were permitted to keep bobtails. Then a plague of rats and mice in the 17th century caused them to be liberated. They spread to the general population, where people came to regard the Mi-Ke (pronounced Mee-Kay and meaning 'three-coloured fur') as the bearers of good fortune. Their popularity was helped by the fact that long-tailed cats were suspected of being able to change into human form and cast spells upon their owners.

Trixie in the Tower of London

In February 1601, Robert Devereux, Earl of Essex and one-time favourite of Queen Elizabeth I, was executed on Tower Green for leading a rebellion against her. His supporter, HENRY WRIOTHESLEY, Earl of Southampton, was extremely lucky to escape the same fate for his part in the plot. Instead, he was IMPRISONED in the Tower of London for two years, during which time he was comforted by the company of his beloved black and white cat, Trixie.

People say that the loyal animal found her own way across London, scaling walls and roofs until she found the chimney to Henry's cell and dropped down inside it. She no doubt helped to keep his cell free of vermin and may even have caught a few pigeons for him.

On his release after Elizabeth's death, Wriothesley, who was also a prominent patron of William Shakespeare, commissioned this unusual PORTRAIT of himself and Trixie, from the painter John de Critz the Elder.

'People say that the loyal animal found her own way across London, scaling walls and roofs until she found the chimney to Henry's cell'

Henry Wriothesley, 3rd Earl of Southampton (1603)
JOHN DE CRITZ THE ELDER
(*c.*1552–1642)

The Ship's Cat

Cats have given rise to more superstitions than any other animal, so it is no surprise that the unpredictable lives of seafarers have led to a whole store of beliefs surrounding the ship's cat. Seamen would avoid using the word 'cat' while at sea, but to have one on board was thought lucky, especially a black one with no white hairs.

GOOD LUCK attended a sailor if the cat ran aboard ahead of him. If it was playful, he would have an easy voyage, but *a meowing cat pointed to future dangers.* Although the main reason for keeping a cat on board was to catch vermin, her wellbeing always seemed inextricably linked to that of both ship and crew; even now, cats are

American sailor holding a cat, the ship's mascot, aboard the destroyer USS Macdonough III (1935)

rarely left on an abandoned ship but are generally rescued with the sailors.

Sailors would watch the cat closely, hoping to PREDICT the WEATHER or the outcome of a voyage. A cat washing its face, or sneezing, foretold rain; licking its fur against the grain, meant a hailstorm. A restless cat with a twitching tail meant a storm was brewing; and actually throwing a cat overboard would raise the wind. *According to tradition, it was certain doom if a cat got into the rigging.* Killing a cat resulted in nine years of bad luck (because of the cat's nine lives), and anybody drowning one risked meeting the same fate himself – in a tempest.

Meanwhile, at home, sailors' wives kept cats to ensure their husbands' safe return.

Faith, the Blitz Cat

Father Henry Ross, rector of St Augustine and St Faith, Watling Street, in the City of London, typed and posted this tribute inside the surviving church tower, where he continued to hold services. Faith was the first cat to be awarded a medal for bravery.

'FAITH'

Our dear little church cat of St Augustine and St Faith. The bravest cat in the world. On Monday, September 9th, 1940, she endured horrors and perils beyond the power of words to tell. Shielding her kitten in a sort of recess in the house (a spot she selected three days before the tragedy occurred), she sat the whole frightful night of bombing and fire, guarding her little kitten. The roofs and masonry exploded. The whole house blazed. Four floors fell through in front of her.

Fire and water and ruin all round her. Yet she stayed calm and steadfast and waited for help. We rescued her in the early morning while the place was still burning, and by the mercy of Almighty God, she and her kitten were not only saved, but unhurt. God be praised and thanked for His goodness and mercy to our dear little pet.

The English Watchcat

In 1922, at a house in Leytonstone, East London, the family cat turned **WATCHDOG** when two burglars attempted a break-in during the early hours of the morning. This clever pet tabby threw himself at the front door and sounded a *rat-a-tat-tat* with the knocker at the letterbox. **THE BURGLARS WERE SCARED OFF** empty handed, and the cat found himself promoted to a place of honour among the family pets.

Dogs Remember Faces, Cats Places

OLD ENGLISH SAYING

Cats have an extraordinary knack of finding their way back to a previous home without any visual clues. Some HOMESICK PETS have travelled literally hundreds of miles and taken as long as a year to make the journey back to where they used to live.

Scientific tests have proved that cats have a high degree of sensitivity to the earth's magnetic field; when experimenters attached strong magnets to cats, they disrupted their homing ability in a way that neither drugs nor any other sensory blocks could do; and it is also thought that they use the angle of the sun as a guide.

This picture, drawn by the author himself, illustrates one of Rudyard Kipling's *Just So Stories for Little Children* (1902), entitled 'The Cat that Walked by Himself'. Kipling's own caption reads: 'WALKING BY HIS WILD LONE THROUGH THE WET WILD WOODS & WAVING HIS WILD TAIL'.

'Scientific tests have proved that cats have a high degree of sensitivity to the earth's magnetic field'

The Cat of Kazan

The Cat of Kazan comes from an 18th-century Russian LUBOK or FOLK PRINT, *which satirizes Tsar Peter the Great and his huge moustache.* These bright, simple woodcuts were coloured by hand and sold everywhere in bazaars and markets; their style is a mixture of traditional European woodcut and Russian icon painting. They became a popular way of expressing people's feelings about daily events, customs, and ideals – as well as decorating their walls – from the mid–17th century until the start of the 20th.

The Cat of Kazan (*18th century*)
PRIVATE COLLECTION

How the Manx Lost her Tail

NOAH was hammering the last nails into the Ark as huge black rain clouds gathered overhead. He knew there was no time to lose and began calling the animals together so that he and his three sons could herd them all aboard.

Now, there was one cat – AN EXCELLENT MOUSER – who was out hunting. She heard Noah's call well enough but she was determined not to go into the Ark without something for her supper.

When Noah had counted the other creatures safely inside, he knew that one was still missing. So he stood in the doorway of the Ark and, as the first drops of rain splashed onto the deck, he shouted:

'Who's out is out and who's in is in!'

He was just closing the door when the cat came running up and squeezed past his ankles in the nick of time. But as Noah

slammed the door, IT CUT OFF HER TAIL, and so the cat got in without it.

And that is why Manx cats have no tails to this day.

Manx Kitten (2007)
BEAU HOOKER

Halloween Greetings

Halloween did not become a holiday in America until the 19th century, where a long-established PURITAN tradition had meant that even Christmas was not much celebrated before the 1800s. It was the potato famine of the 1840s and the migration of the Irish that brought Halloween and its customs to America. The commercialization of Halloween in the United States probably began with Halloween POSTCARDS like this one, which people sent and received between 1905 and 1915.

The black cat became associated with Halloween because of a common belief that the spirits of the dead could return in the shape of an animal – and black cats were certainly one of the most ominous. Witches had also adopted black cats as 'familiars' and so they too became part of the Halloween imagery.

'The black cat became associated with Halloween because of a common belief that the spirits of the dead could return in the shape of an animal'

Hallowe'en Greetings (1910)
FRANCES BRUNDAGE
(1854–1937)

Picture Credits

Bridgeman: 2, 33, 37, 38, 45, 73, 83, 91, 102, 110

Corbis: 7, 8, 13, 15, 22, 31, 35, 57, 59, 65, 67, 77, 79, 81, 87, 93, 97, 107, 113, 115, 116, 119

Mary Evans: 11, 17, 21, 28, 42–43, 46, 49, 69, 71, 89, 105, 109, 118, 121

Picture Desk (Art Archive): 16, 19, 25, 26, 41, 75, 85, 99, 123, 127

Shutterstock: 4, 51, 61

Photograph on p 125 reproduced with the kind permission of Beau Hooker

Acknowledgements

The traditional tales on pp 12, 54 and 124 were retold by Charlotte Gerlings